FOR CLEMENTINE AND HER GRANDMAMA —B. H.

Henry Holt and Company
Publishers since 1866
115 West 18th Street, New York, New York 10011

Text copyright © 1999 by Frances Lincoln Limited
Photographs copyright ©1999 by Oxfam Activities Limited and
the photographers as named
All rights reserved.
First published in the United States in 1999
by Henry Holt and Company.
Originally published in the United Kingdom in 1999
by Frances Lincoln Limited.

Library of Congress Catalog Card Number: 99-60655

ISBN 0-8050-6293-9
First American edition—1999

Illustrated by Diane Lilley
Designed by Sarah Slack

Printed in Hong Kong

10 9 8 7 6 5 4 3 2 1

Oxfam and the publishers would like to thank all the children who took part in *Wake Up, World!*, and their families and communities for their enthusiastic support. Oxfam commissioned photographers from around the world to visit the eight children featured in the book and, together with the publishers, would like to thank them:

Howard Davies took the photographs of Paige in Brighton, UK.

Sarah Errington traveled to western Siberia to visit Sasha and his family, followed by a trip to Ghana to Anusibuno's village.

Julio Etchart visited Ludovico village in Brazil to meet Cidinha and her family.

Jim Holmes took the photographs of Linh in Ky Anh, Vietnam.

Rajendra Shaw lives and works in Hyderabad, India. He took the photographs of Shakeel.

Sean Sprague visited Natali at her home in California, USA.

Penny Tweedie took the photographs of Alexis and her friends in Alice Springs, Australia.

Oxfam will receive a 5 percent royalty for each copy of this book sold in the US.
Oxfam is a Registered Charity no. 202918.

Oxfam believes every human being is entitled to a life of dignity and opportunity. Working with others we use our ingenuity, knowledge, and wealth of experience to make resources and money work harder. From practical work with individuals to influencing world policy we enable the world's poorest people to create a future that no longer needs Oxfam.

Wake Up, World!

A Day in the Life of Children Around the World

BEATRICE HOLLYER

With an introduction by Tony Robinson

Henry Holt and Company • New York

In Association with Oxfam

I have a friend called Cidinha, who cracks a hundred nuts every day—they're the size of apples, with shells as hard as a very hard math problem. They grow on trees around her village.

Cidinha is seven years old. You may think she's quite different from you—and I'm not just talking about the nut-cracking. Her house is made of mud and leaves. She sleeps in a hammock. She's never played a computer game or waited in line for a burger. So, she is very different from you, isn't she?

Well maybe, but maybe not. She has a gang of friends (just like you) who go to their own special places and tell each other secrets. She knows all the latest pop songs. She's sometimes picked on by her older brothers and sisters, and she doesn't think it's fair when she has to go to bed earlier than they do. All that's a bit like you, isn't it?

So why does she crack nuts? Well, everyone in her village does. Before Cidinha was born, farmers tried to drive her family and friends out of their village so that they could take over the land. Everyone was scared, but they stayed put and they stayed together. They wanted to make their lives better. Nuts grew all around them, so they set up a factory that uses oil from them to make soap, which they can sell. Cidinha is proud of the soap factory. Nut-cracking is her part in making the village better.

In lots of ways Cidinha's life is very different from yours, but it's also similar. And that's true of children all over the world. We're going to tell you eight stories about children from all four corners of the globe. Some of their lives may seem a little strange to you, but remember there are some things we have in common. They all like to stay up late, they all like sweets, they all moan when they're not allowed to go out and play, and they all get scolded about sixteen times a day. And that's definitely like you, isn't it?

Tony Robinson

Our

My name is **PAIGE**. It was my grandmother's last name before she was married, and it's my mother's middle name. I live in Brighton in the **UNITED KINGDOM**.

My name is **NATALI,** which means "born at Christmas." My middle name, Xochiquetzal (zo-ki-kwet-zal), is the name of the Mexican goddess of spring. I live in Berkeley, California, in the **UNITED STATES OF AMERICA**.

My name is Aparecida (a-pa-re-thi-da), but everyone calls me **CIDINHA** (shid-jin-ya). I live in Ludovico village in **BRAZIL**.

My name is **ANUSIBUNO** (an-oo-si-boo-no), which means "things of my hand." I live in Zuo village in **GHANA**.

World

My name is **SASHA**. It is short for Alexandr, which means "winner." I live in Lekarstvennoye village in **RUSSIA**.

My name is **LINH** (ling). We put our family names first, then our first names, so my full name is Hoang Xuan Linh (hon zu-an ling). I live in Ky Anh in **VIETNAM**.

My name is **ALEXIS**. My last name, Abala, is an Aboriginal name. I live in Alice Springs in **AUSTRALIA**.

My name is Mohammad Shakeel, although everyone knows me as **SHAKEEL**. It means "handsome." I live in Hyderabad in **INDIA**.

Wake up!

The moment we open our eyes to a new day is something we all share. But what we see, feel, and hear around us is different, depending on where we live.

"I like to sleep late in my hammock. It's so comfortable that my mother has to shake me awake. In the room where I sleep we store rice in big sacks."—**Cidinha**

Alexis's house has four bedrooms. Her room has bunk beds, and she sleeps in the top bunk. After her mother wakes her, Alexis makes her bed before climbing down for breakfast.

Shakeel and his brother, Shabeer, sleep until their mother wakes them. Their bed is a mattress on the floor. An electric fan blows cool air over them.

As she wakes up, Anusibuno stretches on the sleeping mat she shares with her mother and four sisters. When it's hot, they move the mat and sleep outside.

"It's dark and cold outside when I wake up. Our cat, Pushok, keeps me warm. He is like a fluffy blanket."—**Sasha**

 Natali wakes herself up with her alarm clock. Once she's awake, she reads or pretends her bed is a zoo, full of her toy animals.

 When Linh wakes up, he lifts the mosquito net that covers the bed he shares with his mother, father, and brother. They sleep, eat, and watch television in the same room.

 Paige cuddles her toy monkey as she gets up. Her bedroom is painted pink, her favorite color. She likes to watch TV while her parents are still asleep.

Who else is awake?

When we wake up, we look around and see who else is up and about. We say "Good morning!" to people and animals who share our homes. All over the world, children live with their parents, brothers and sisters, and sometimes grandparents, aunts, uncles, or cousins. Pets and other animals are part of family life, too.

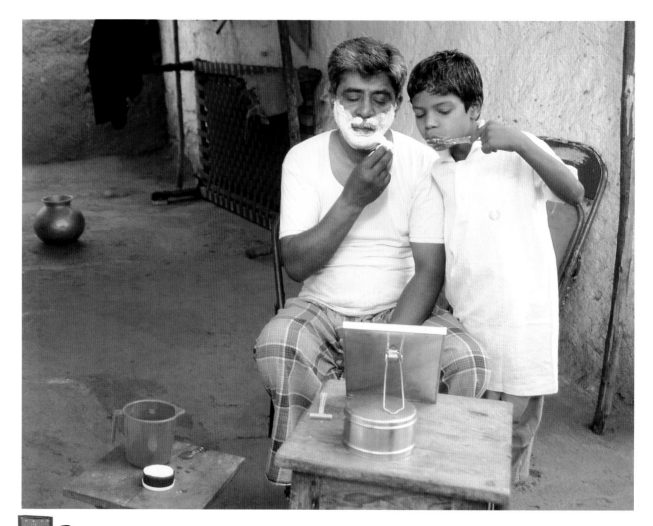

Before Shakeel wakes up, his mother brings water from the tap on the road, so that he and his father can wash. Together they set up a small table and a mirror in the courtyard of their house. Shakeel brushes his teeth while he watches his father shave.

The pigs and chickens are waiting for their breakfast when Cidinha wakes up. Her mother has lit the stove, brought water from the well, and made coffee for everyone. She calls Cidinha to feed the animals. Her father and big brother have already left for work in the fields.

Alexis likes to see all her toys at the end of her bed. She pretends they are waiting for her to wake up. Her mother is busy getting her five brothers and sisters ready for school.

Every morning Sasha is up early, helping to dress his younger sister, Yulya, and make breakfast. His stepfather is away working, so Sasha takes pride in being the man of the house, helping his mother and *babushka* (Russian for grandmother) in every way he can.

"My mother wakes up at dawn because she has so much to do before she starts work in the fields. Then my father gets up and goes to work, leaving lots of space in our family bed. My brother is still asleep when I start doing my homework."—**Linh**

★ Natali and her older sister, Ali, like to spend time together in the bathroom after they wake up, brushing their teeth, chatting, and looking in the mirror. They sometimes forget that their parents and uncle also need to use the bathroom!

🏠 "I get up before everyone else and help myself to a drink, because I can't wait to start the day. If Mum and Dad are still asleep, my sister and I play with my hamster, Hamish. He's nocturnal, so he's been awake most of the night."—**Paige**

Anusibuno wakes up with her parents, four sisters, and twenty-four other relations. They share a compound, a collection of rooms in a walled yard. Her father and the other men get up first, to let out the animals to graze in the open until night falls.

Starting the day

Between waking up and setting off for school, children around the world eat breakfast, wash, brush their teeth, and get dressed. In hot countries, they wake up with a quick splash of cool water, and pull on a pair of shorts. In cold climates, everything takes longer; no one wants to get out of a warm bed and then put on layers of clothes to brave the cold outside.

"I shower, dress, then help myself to breakfast—cereal, orange juice, and yogurt—which I eat with my sisters. My little brother is still asleep and my big brother has already left for school on his bicycle." When Alexis goes out, she has to remember to wear her hat, to protect herself from the burning sun.

Anusibuno washes in the water she has carried from the well. Afterward, she rubs shea butter onto her skin, to protect it from the wind and sun. She would love to wear brightly colored clothes, but she has only one skirt and T-shirt, which she wears every day for school. For breakfast, she eats *pumpuka*, millet porridge, sometimes with smoked fish and spices.

On school days, Paige prepares breakfast for herself and her sister. They have a choice of cereals, then toast with peanut butter. After breakfast, Paige brushes her teeth before deciding what to wear.

Sasha boils water for tea while his mother fries potatoes. For a treat, he sometimes has milk and bread and butter for breakfast. Before he goes out in the snow, he puts on an extra sweater, padded jacket and trousers, felt boots, mittens, a scarf, and a fur hat.

"For breakfast, we eat *parathas*, bread fried in oil, and we drink tea— I add lots of sugar to mine! We eat in the courtyard, just outside the kitchen. Afterward Ammy (Mommy) helps me get ready for school. I like wearing new clothes, and I look forward to festival days when we get clothes as presents."—**Shakeel**

Cidinha washes with soap made from babassu nuts. The water comes from a deep well. It still has some earth in it, but it's soft and cool. After her bucket shower, she has coffee mixed with manioc flour, made from the cassava plant. Breakfast is indoors because it's hot and dusty outside.

"I often wear my favorite sweater, handed down from Ali. The dogs on it remind me of my grandparents' dog, Farley. Ali lets me borrow her earrings and helps me to put them on. Once I'm dressed, I eat breakfast, usually toasted bagels and cereal."—**Natali**

After he's done his homework, Linh washes rice for his mother to cook with fish and vegetables for breakfast. When he has finished eating, he brushes his teeth while perched on the wall outside his house so that he can see what everyone else is doing.

Off to school!

When children go to school, they step outside their homes and families to new places among children of their own ages. Depending on where they live, children make the journey in different ways. For some, it's a long walk, with a chance to play along the way; others ride in a bus, train, or car.

Natali's uncle walks her to school. When it rains, they go by car. After school starts, the gates are locked to keep the children safe.

"School is only two minutes away. It takes Mum longer to get us all into the car than it does to drive there!"—**Alexis**

Linh walks to school at midday, when it is extremely hot. He always remembers his satchel, but sometimes he forgets his hat.

Anusibuno shares bags of nuts with her friends on their half-hour walk to school. They like to hang around the water pump, chatting, until the grown-ups shout "Hurry or you'll be late!"

"I ride to school in my father's auto-rickshaw, a taxi with three wheels. I see lots of monkeys on the way."—**Shakeel**

"I walk to school alone. It's quiet and beautiful. I look at the different-colored houses—red, yellow, and green—and I see how beautiful they are. "—**Sasha**

If it's wet, Paige goes to school by car. On the way, she looks out for the chestnut tree in the churchyard, where she collects chestnuts in autumn.

Cidinha's house is between the village shop and the open space where the children play football. Her school is just a short walk away, straight down the same red dirt road.

At school

Everywhere in the world, school is important. While we learn about children in other countries, they are learning about us. A school may have lots of classrooms, books, equipment, and a playground, or lessons may take place under trees.

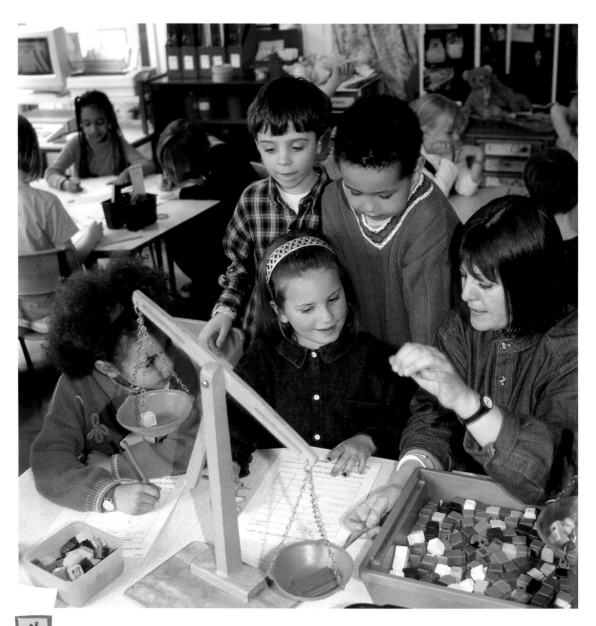

"We are learning to work out how much things weigh while other children are reading and drawing." Paige and her friends started school in the nursery class when they were three years old.

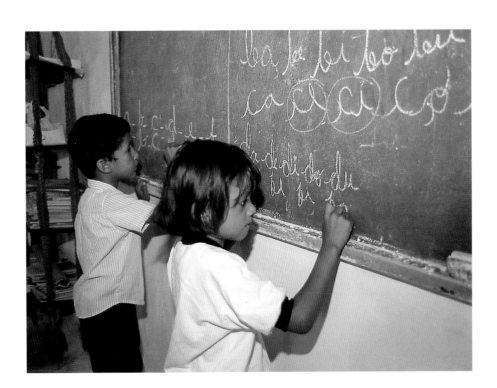

"I like wearing these clothes because they show that I go to school. Not everyone goes to school, so I feel lucky, especially when I learn how to write a new word."
—Cidinha

Children in Vietnam have to share the school day because there are not enough schools or teachers. Linh goes to school in the afternoons. When he arrives, he does exercises called *duc* with the whole school in the shade of the trees the children have planted.

Linh and his friends plant and water new trees to give shade and protect the soil from floods.

"I like to be the first in the classroom and surprise the others when they arrive. There are only nine children in my class today because some of them think it is too cold to go out. The temperature outside is minus forty-four degrees Fahrenheit! Today we're practicing the alphabet."
—**Sasha**

 "My best friend, Jordan, and I are using the internet to share news with schoolchildren in other parts of Australia. Sometimes we play computer games, too."—**Alexis**

 Anusibuno calls herself Mary at school, the same name as her teacher. She helps to sweep the classrooms and the yard before lessons start. She shares her class with younger children, so it's quite crowded. Sometimes her friends don't come to school because they have to help their parents at home.

⭐ At Natali's school, the children work on their own, sitting in groups at separate tables. The teacher talks to them one by one. Everyone has a special box with his name on it for his own projects, pens, and pencils. Natali enjoys silent reading and writing stories.

🌸 Shakeel wears a blue-and-white school uniform. It's hot and dusty, and some of the children go barefoot. Their teacher wears a traditional sari. In art class, she sits cross-legged on the mats with them. Shakeel is printing with a vegetable called okra. He decorates his painting with dried lentils.

Playtime!

Children all over the world use what they find around them to invent games, try out new ideas, make their own toys, and have fun. Some children work hard to help their families. Others have lots of homework. But there's always time for play.

Ludovico, the village where Cidinha lives, is hot, dusty, and dry. It has one dirt road, lined with houses made of earth. When Cidinha and her friends play football or their favorite skipping game, *elástico*, they kick up clouds of red dust. They cool off by swimming and splashing for hours in the lake. They don't have toys, but an old bicycle wheel makes a good hoop!

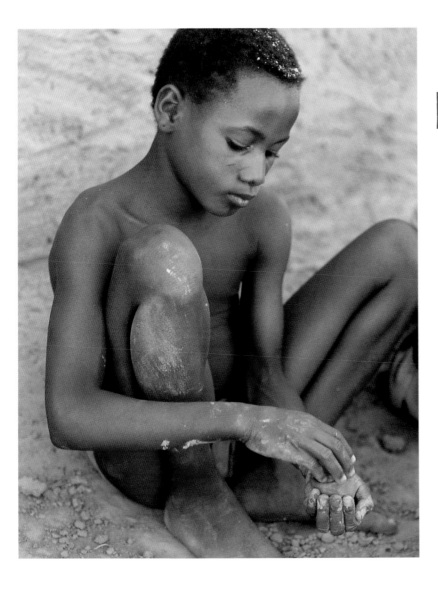

"I play with my sisters and other relatives. There are eighteen children living in the same compound, so someone is always ready to join in the fun. We mark out squares in the earth to play hopscotch and make toys and people from clay. We leave them to dry in the sun and then we play with them."
—**Anusibuno**

"I love Hamish, my hamster. I play with him every day. We also have two goldfish: Freddie is mine and Bug is my sister Bobbie's." Paige likes drawing, too. Her kitchen wall is covered with her pictures.

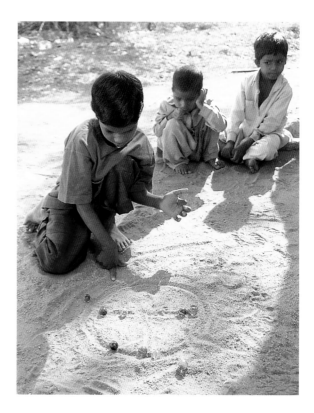

Shakeel draws tracks for his marbles in the dry, sandy earth. His friends are wearing long cotton tunics, called *kurta*, to keep cool.

Like most children in rural Vietnam, Linh has no toys but makes up his own games. His favorite game is *vong*. Each player uses rubber bands to shoot pebbles at a target. The winner (the person who hits the target) keeps the rubber bands.

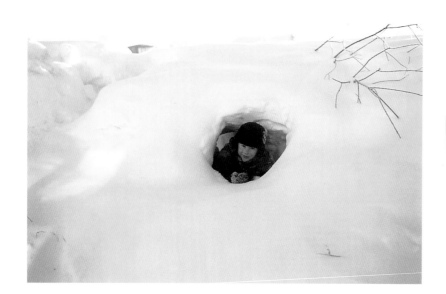

"I make houses in the snow. When I work from dawn to dusk, I can almost finish a house in a day. I smooth the walls, inside and out. If the snow is damp and sticky, I make little tables, beds, and chairs."—**Sasha**

Natali practices the piano with her mother every day after school. She enjoys playing, but she would rather read or watch videos eating take-out pizza. She has lots of toys, games, and books of her own. At the moment, she's reading a book called *California Girl*.

The sun is blazing hot in Alice Springs where Alexis lives. After school, she and her friends ride their bicycles to the pool or play basketball. Alexis also likes watching television and listening to music.

Helping others

Because we share our lives with the people around us, we have to help one another in all sorts of ways. Doing special jobs for our families is an important part of growing up. Whether we set the table, tidy our toys, or look after animals, it can be fun to share the work at home.

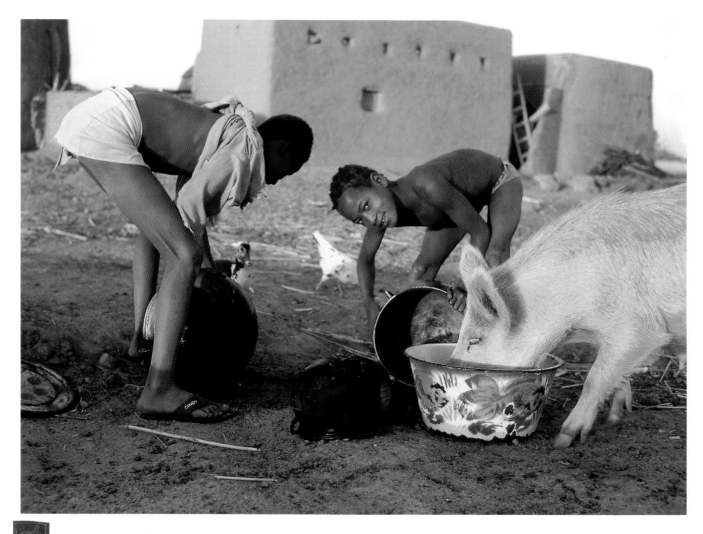

"Every day, I sweep the rooms and fetch firewood. My sister and I like washing the cooking pots and dishes, because when we've done them, they are clean for visitors. They can see how much we help our mother, and we feel proud."—**Anusibuno**

Every two days, Sasha and his brother, Vanya, collect water from the well. They pull the heavy canisters on a sled. Sasha also clears snow from the path, brings in logs for the fire, and helps with the ·cooking. He is especially good at making meat dumplings, called *pelmeni*.

Paige's favorite job is cleaning her hamster's cage. "I like taking care of Hamish. I give him fresh sawdust and water. The job I like least is carrying my toys and clothes back up to my room from downstairs, as there are so many stairs to climb!"

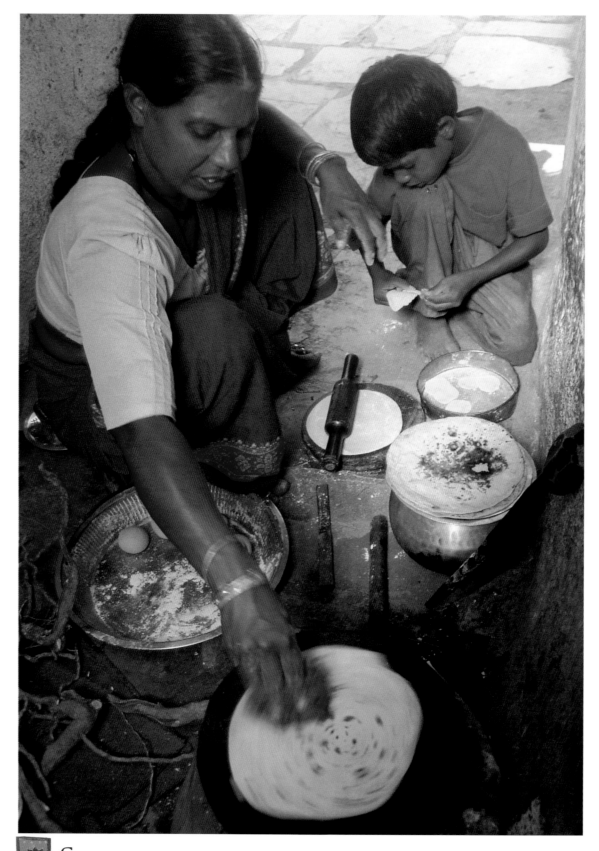

Shakeel helps his mother make flat bread, called *chapatis,* outside the kitchen. He helps his father with building work when their house needs repairs. Shakeel's own job is feeding and milking the goats. When he is older, he would like to do the shopping and carry the heavy bags for his mother.

Linh's special job is feeding rice to the chickens twice a day. His family keeps pigs as well, but Linh stays away from them because he doesn't like the noise they make.

"Cooking is the job I like best. I mix things and then lick the spoon. That's lots of fun, but I don't enjoy cleaning up afterward."—**Natali**

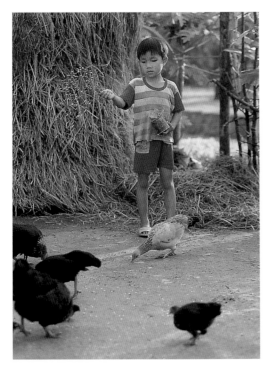

Alexis helps sort her dirty clothes into whites and colors. She puts them in the washing machine and then hangs them out to dry in the sun.

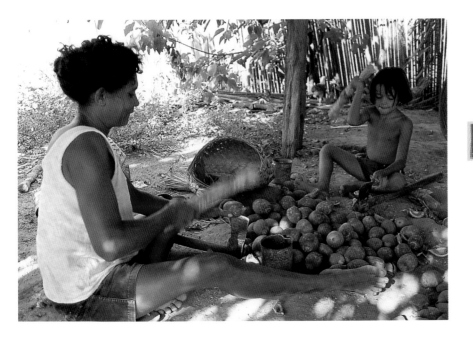

Cidinha helps her mother break babassu nuts. The oil in the nuts is valuable because the villagers use it to make soap, which they sell. Cidinha can exchange the cracked nuts at the village shop for a new pencil case or a notebook.

Time to eat!

Everyplace in the world has its own special food and different ways of cooking and eating. Some people can choose from many types of food; others eat the same meals nearly every day and hardly ever have sweets or treats. Children everywhere love to eat because food tastes good, and it helps them to grow big and strong.

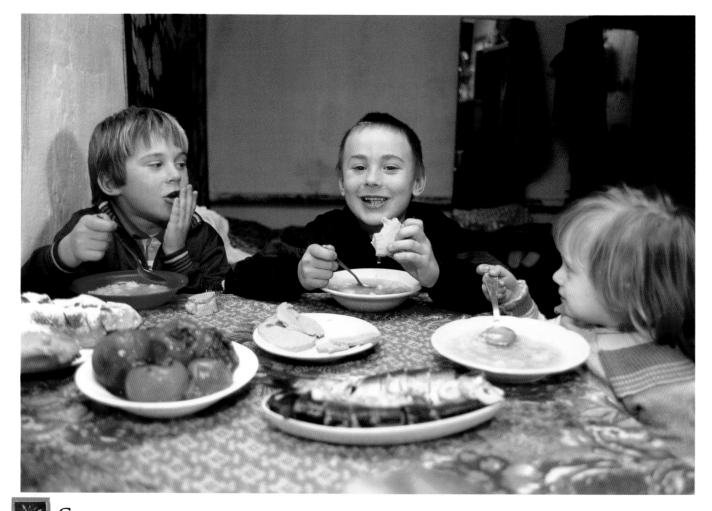

Sasha's family eat their main meal, called *obed*, in the afternoon. They start with soup made from vegetables grown in their garden and then they eat pickled fish, ham, stuffed tomatoes, and pastries. They need lots of food to keep them warm in the freezing winter. Sasha's favorite meal is *borscht*, a soup made from beets.

In Vietnam even small children are expert at using chopsticks. Dinner is called *bua toi*. The main part of the meal is rice, with small dishes of fish and vegetables. Linh's family grows rice and vegetables in their own fields. Sometimes they buy pork, Linh's favorite dish, from their neighbor.

Cidinha's family and neighbors crowd into the living room of her house to watch TV while they have dinner, called *janta*. They eat rice and beans flavored with spring onion and coriander, which they grow themselves. Meat comes from their own chickens and pigs. Sometimes they eat fish that Cidinha's father and brothers have caught in the lake.

Anusibuno eats porridge made with corn or millet for every meal. She and her sisters sit outdoors, sharing bowls and eating with the fingers of one hand. She likes *bito*, a soup made with leafy vegetables and nuts, which they grow themselves.

Once a week Paige has her favorite meal of roasted meat or chicken with roasted potatoes, vegetables, and gravy. On other days she might eat pasta with tuna fish, fish sticks, or salads. When Paige invites school friends home for tea, they have chocolate cookies as a treat.

Shakeel tears *chapatis*—soft, flat bread—into pieces and uses them to scoop up rice and *dal*, a lentil stew. Most days his mother cooks vegetables in a spicy curry sauce. Shakeel looks forward to Sundays when they have meat curry, called *gosht*.

"I go to my grandmother's house for tea on Friday nights with all my cousins. We eat pasta and barbecue in the garden. My favorite food is take-out hamburgers. We have them for lunch at school on Fridays and once a week for tea at home."—**Alexis**

Natali enjoys salads made from the fruit and vegetables that grow in hot, sunny California. Everyone in the family has a choice of salad dressing and a choice of milk or fruit juice to drink. Once a month, for a treat, they eat take-out pizza, which Natali's mother orders by telephone.

Time for bed

At nighttime, we rest our minds and bodies before we wake up to another busy day. As evening comes, we start to feel sleepy and look forward to bed, whether we sleep on a mat, in a hammock, bunk, or family bed.

 "I pretend I'm a Martian in the silver pajamas Mommy made me. She blesses me and kisses me before I fall asleep."—**Sasha**

Shakeel goes to sleep either listening to his sister reading stories or watching TV. He has a favorite pillow that he doesn't like anyone else to use.

Before Paige goes to bed, she reads a story with her mother or father, or plays a game. She cuddles up with her toy monkey and then her parents say good night.

It's hot at night, so Cidinha often sleeps in just a pair of shorts. Before she goes to sleep, her sister or her mother reads to her, or they look over her schoolwork.

"After my parents kiss me good night, I go to sleep with my most cuddly bear, Chester Junior." Natali likes to keep special toys and photos around her bed.

lexis goes to bed late. "Some nights I have a shower, then I read comics to myself before Mum comes for a hug and kiss."

"I go to bed as it gets dark, when the frogs start croaking. The last thing I do is get the pillow and pull down the mosquito net. We don't need a blanket until the morning, when it gets cold."—**Linh**

"After supper, my sisters bring out the sleeping mat. We tell each other stories and sing songs as we lie in the dark. I listen to the sounds of animals and people and drift off to sleep."
—**Anusibuno**

In my dreams

Our dreams take us to places different from our everyday lives. When children dream at night, they tell themselves stories while they sleep. Daydreams are what they wish for when they are awake: peace in the world, a visit to the moon, a day at the beach, or a new toy. They especially wonder what life will be like when they grow up, and dream about what they will do in the future.

"My dream is to be a vet, and have a horse of my own. I want to fly around the world to see different creatures that live in faraway places. The world might be quite different when I grow up, but I'll always love animals."—**Paige**

"In my dreams, I go into the stories I've been reading and watching on TV. I become part of them, a princess or a character from a film. When I grow up, I want to be like Pocahontas, strong and fast, brave, and loyal."
—**Natali**

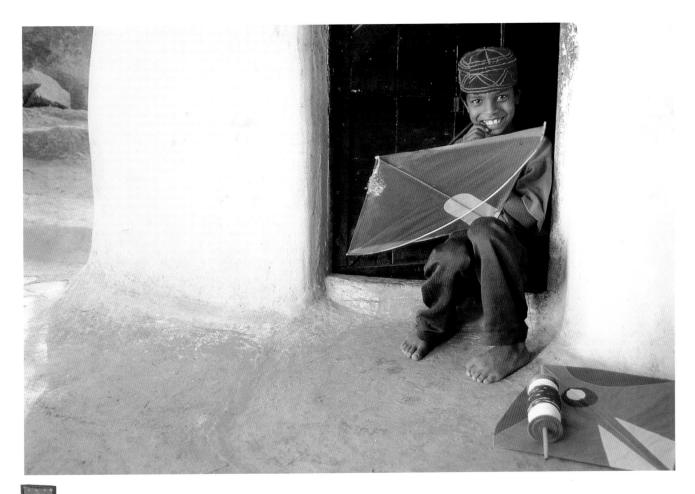

"I never remember the dreams I have when I'm asleep, but when I'm awake, whatever I'm doing, I dream of a brand-new bicycle, with shiny mud guards and brakes that work."
—**Shakeel**

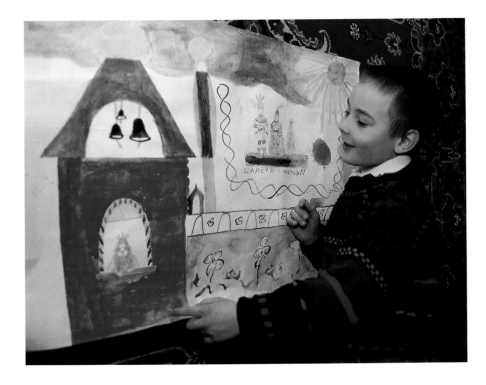

"In my dreams, our house is turned into the Kingdom of Happiness, where Mommy is queen, my sister is a princess, and my brother a prince. I am the head of the kingdom. There is a singing firebird with sparkling feathers that shine at night."—**Sasha**

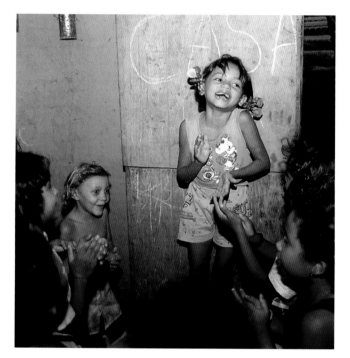

"One day, I'd like to be a famous singer and dancer. For now, I wish I could have a doll. Sometimes I dream I'm sitting in the shade by a well and playing with a doll; sometimes I dream about the sea."—**Cidinha**

"I often dream I'm meeting the musicians in my favorite band. They sing for me and talk to me. In real life, when I grow up I will travel the world, listening to music everywhere I go."—**Alexis**

"I dream of the day when our house is finished. When I grow up, I want to be a builder like my father. People will pay me to build houses for them, and I will use the money to build a home for my own family."
—**Linh**

"I dream of being a teacher when I grow up, or perhaps a photographer. I'd like to take pictures of ordinary people doing their everyday work and of children playing."—**Anusibuno**

Ghana

Anusibuno lives in Ghana on the west coast of Africa, the second largest continent in the world. In the south of Ghana, there are cities, forests, and farmland. The capital, Accra, is modern and bustling. In the north, where Anusibuno lives, it is dry. Fewer people live there, and life is slower and more traditional. Many people have to carry their water from the village well and use kerosene lamps for light and cook over a wood fire. Everyone shares the work in the compound where Anusibuno lives: children help to pound millet and corn to make porridge, and look after animals.

Anusibuno uses an English name at school. Besides her native language, Kasena nankani, Anusibuno also speaks English, because Ghana was once ruled by Britain. Today all the countries of Africa are independent.

India

Shakeel lives in Hyderabad in India, the second most populated country in the world, after China. Hyderabad is hot and arid, but other areas in India are green and lush.

Parts of India are modern, with hundreds of factories producing computers, cars, and electronics. The biggest cities, Calcutta, Delhi, and Bombay, are very crowded. However, three-quarters of India's people work outside the cities, on the land, growing most of the world's tea and cotton.

Ancient traditions and customs of different religions—Islam, Hinduism, Sikhism, Christianity, and Buddhism—are part of everyday life for most Indians. Shakeel is a Muslim. He speaks Urdu, one of sixteen languages spoken in India. The main ones are Hindi and English.

Russia

Sasha lives in Siberia, which makes up most of Russia, the biggest nation in the world. Although Siberia covers a large area, not many people live there because of the extreme cold in winter. Northern Siberia is inside the Arctic Circle, not far from the North Pole. In some places, the snow never melts and even the sea is frozen. Sometimes the cold can freeze your breath.

In summer people spend much more time outdoors. They grow vegetables and grain on their farms. Sasha's village is well known for its crops of camomile flowers, which Sasha helps pick to make tea and medicine that the villagers can sell.

Many Siberians work in coal mines or producing timber from the forests. Others go to the cities to find work. Sasha's stepfather works in Novosibirsk, the capital of Siberia.

Australia

Alexis lives in Alice Springs in Australia, the only country that is also a continent. Australia is an enormous island with animals, such as the koala and the kangaroo, that are found nowhere else in the world.

The first Australians were Aboriginals, like Alexis's father and grandmother. In the last century, people from all over Asia and Europe have settled in Australia. They are attracted by the warm, sunny weather and the outdoor life of beaches, picnics, and barbecues.

Most people live on the coast, in and around the main cities of Canberra (the capital), Sydney, Perth, and Melbourne. Alice Springs is in the Australian outback, the flat, semidesert region in the heart of the country. The best-known feature of central Australia is Ayers Rock. People travel from all over the world to see this huge outcrop of red sandstone in the middle of the desert.